S0-BRJ-106

DISCARDED

Public Library
Incorporated 1925
Barrie Ontario

Gandhi
The Peaceful Revolutionary

Anna Claybourne

RAINTREE
STECK-VAUGHN
PUBLISHERS

A Harcourt Company

Austin   New York
www.raintreesteckvaughn.com

Public Library
incorporated 1862
Barrie, Ontario

Titles in this series:
Muhammad Ali: The Greatest
Neil Armstrong: The First Man on the Moon
Fidel Castro: Leader of Cuba's Revolution
Anne Frank: Voice of Hope
Gandhi: The Peaceful Revolutionary
Bill Gates: Computer Legend
Martin Luther King, Jr.: Civil Rights Hero
The Dalai Lama: Peacemaker from Tibet
John Lennon: Musician with a Message
Nelson Mandela: Father of Freedom
Florence Nightingale: The Lady of the Lamp
Pope John Paul II: Pope for the People
Queen Elizabeth II: Monarch of Our Times
The Queen Mother: Grandmother of a Nation

Copyright 2003, text, Steck-Vaughn Company

All rights reserved. No part of this book may be reproduced or utilized in any form or by any means, electronic or mechanical, including photocopying, recording, or by any information storage and retrieval system, without permission in writing from the Publishers. Inquiries should be addressed to:

Copyright Permissions, Steck-Vaughn Company,
P.O. Box 26015, Austin, TX 78755.

Published by Raintree Steck-Vaughn Publishers,
an imprint of Steck-Vaughn Company

Library of Congress Cataloging-in-Publication Data

Claybourne, Anna.
    Gandhi/Anna Claybourne.
        p. cm.—(Famous Lives)
    Summary: A biography of the gentle but stubborn man who called on
    Indians to disobey British laws through civil disobediance and non-
    cooperation until India was granted independence.
    Includes bibiliographical references and index.
    ISBN 0-7398-5521-2
    1. Gandhi, Mahatma, 1869-1948—Juvenile literature. 2. India—Politics
and government—1919-1947—Juvenile literature. 3. Nationalists—
India—Biography—Juvenile literature. [1. Gandhi, Mahatma, 1869-1948.
2. Statesmen. 3. India—Politics and government—1919-1947.] I. Title. II.
Famous lives (Austin, Tex.)

DS481.G3 C5516 2003
954.03'5'092—dc21
                                                            2002019701

Printed in Italy. Bound in the United States.

1 2 3 4 5 6 7 8 9 0 LB 07 06 05 04 03 02

Cover: Gandhi photographed in 1941
Title page: Gandhi in South Africa in 1914

Picture acknowledgments
The publisher would like to thank the following for their kind permission to use these pictures:AKG 11; AP 32; British Library, London/Bridgeman Art Library 8; Camera Press 27 (bottom); Corbis (cover),19, 25, 33; Hodder Wayland Picture Library 15, 21, 36; Hulton Deutsch 28 (bottom), 29; Hulton Getty 12, 17, 30; Illustrated London News Picture Library 39; Images of India 23, 45; Paul Popper 40, 44; Popperfoto 7, 14, 22, 24, 26, 27 (top), 28 (top), 31, 35 (bottom), 37, 42, 43; Topham Picturepoint (title page) 4, 5, 6, 9, 10, 13, 16, 18, 20, 34, 35 (top), 41. The map on page 38 is by Tim Mayer.

Contents

A Handful of Salt

It is April 6 ,1930, and the sun is beating down on the beach at Dandi, on India's west coast. A small, thin, 60-year-old man wearing a white robe, wire-rimmed glasses, and simple sandals walks toward the sea, leading thousands of followers. As they reach the water's edge, the man crouches and picks up a handful of salt left there by the evaporating sea water.

"Mass civil disobedience is like an earthquake." Gandhi describing the powerful effects of a people choosing to disobey their rulers.

Gandhi gathers the first handful of salt on the beach at Dandi. He was breaking the law forbidding Indians to collect their own salt.

Picking up salt from a beach may seem an unremarkable act. Yet that day on the beach at Dandi was a turning point in India's history. The man picking up salt was Mohandas K. Gandhi, known as Mahatma, or "Great Soul." By collecting salt he was defying the British leaders who ruled India at the time. They had passed a law that Indians could not collect their own salt, but had to buy it at a high price.

Gandhi called on all Indians to disobey British laws until India was granted independence. Instead of violent riots, he believed in civil disobedience—a calm, peaceful refusal to cooperate with the government. His ideas were to change India, and the world, forever.

A photograph of Mahatma Gandhi in 1931, wearing his simple white robe.

Born in the British Empire

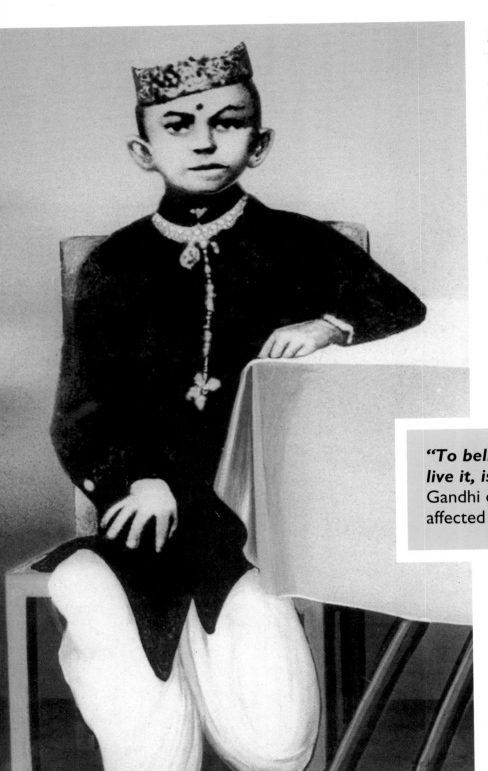

Mohandas Gandhi was born in Porbandar, on the northwest coast of India, in 1869. He was the youngest of four children. Gandhi's father was the prime minister of Porbandar state, a tiny traditional kingdom, and his family was reasonably well off. However, they belonged to the *Vaishya* caste, which is one of the lower social groups in traditional Indian society.

"To believe in something, and not to live it, is dishonest."
Gandhi explaining how his beliefs affected the way he lived his life.

Mohandas Gandhi, at the age of about seven. He showed his gentle yet stubborn nature early in life.

In 1869, India was part of the British Empire. The British made the laws, ran the government, and took India's natural riches for themselves. There were many little kingdoms like Porbandar, but they too were under British control.

While he was growing up, Gandhi was deeply affected by his mother's Hindu religion and by the traditions of Porbandar. Hindus, who believe in many gods, are mostly vegetarian, and some also believe it is wrong to harm any living thing. As a child, Gandhi climbed mango trees in the garden to put bandages on bruised fruits.

This photograph from the days of the British Empire shows two British men having tea in India, attended by three Indian servants.

7

An Early Marriage

"Two innocent children . . . hurled together into the ocean of life."
Gandhi recalling how unprepared he and his wife were for their marriage at the age of 13.

In 1882, when he was only 13, Gandhi was married to a girl chosen by his family. It was a traditional Hindu wedding. The girl's name was Kasturbai Makanji and she was the daughter of a Porbandar clothseller.

Later in his life, Gandhi said that his marrying so young had not been a very good idea. He was too young and wasn't sure how to be a good husband. Like any teenager, he enjoyed spending a lot of time with his friends. Although he was a bright student, he did very poorly at school during the first year of his marriage.

This painting from around 1887 shows a traditional Hindu wedding.

When he was 16, two events changed Gandhi's life. His beloved father, Karamchand Gandhi, died after a long illness, and Gandhi never forgave himself for not being at his father's bedside. Soon afterward, Kasturbai gave birth to their first child. Sadly, the baby died only a few days later. Gandhi realized it was time to grow up and start taking his education seriously.

A 14-year-old Gandhi (left) with a friend.

An English Education

In 1888, when Gandhi was 18, he went to London, England, to study law. Friends and family donated money for the trip so that young Mohandas could have a good education and possibly follow in his father's footsteps as the next prime minister of Porbandar. Gandhi left behind his wife, his baby son Harilal, and his anxious mother. She was worried that her son would eat meat and drink alcohol, which are both forbidden to Hindus. Gandhi promised her he would remain true to his religion.

At first Gandhi was very shy, but he soon began to enjoy British life. He spent money on expensive Western suits and bow ties, had his hair cut in an English style, and learned English manners.

Gandhi (bottom right), dressed in Western clothes, with members of the Vegetarian Society in London. Gandhi made some good friends among members of the society.

"The Gita is not only my Bible or my Koran, it is more than that, it is my mother."
Gandhi describing the *Bhagavadgita*, which he called the *Gita*.

However, after about two years he returned to his Indian roots. He read the *Bhagavadgita*, an ancient Hindu text that urges the faithful to give up material things. He began to live as cheaply as possible, eating the simplest food and walking instead of taking buses. In 1891, Gandhi returned to India, a fully qualified lawyer.

An illustration from a Hindu holy book, the Bhagavata-Purana. While in London, Gandhi studied the ancient Hindu texts of his homeland.

11

An African Adventure

Back in India, Gandhi had trouble finding a job. He moved to Bombay to look for work, with little luck. Life became even more difficult when he tried to become involved in a court case concerning his brother, Laxmidas, and offended a British official. When a law firm in South Africa wrote to offer him a job for a year, he had no choice but to accept.

Gandhi sailed to South Africa in April 1893. When he arrived he took a train to Pretoria to start his new job. During the journey, a white man objected to his presence in a first-class carriage and had him thrown off the train. Left to shiver on an empty station platform all night, Gandhi resolved to fight for the rights of Indians in South Africa.

A steam train emerges from a tunnel in South Africa in 1889. The British brought steam railways to many parts of the British Empire. Indians often worked on the railroads in South Africa.

12

While continuing his legal work, Gandhi began campaigning for better conditions for South Africa's many Indian workers. He soon brought his family from India, and stayed in Africa for more than 20 years.

In 1899, the Boer War broke out between British and Dutch settlers in South Africa. Like many Indians, Gandhi joined the war effort on the British side.

"I discovered that as a man and as an Indian I had no rights."
Gandhi on his first encounter with racial discrimination in South Africa.

Gandhi (middle row, center) in the Indian Ambulance Corps during the Boer War (1899–1902).

Campaigning for Indians

In the 1890s, South Africa, like India, was a part of the British Empire, and many Indians went to work there. However, they were often treated with disrespect. As well as being banned from traveling first-class, they were insulted with racist nicknames, had an evening curfew, and could not vote. They were also forced to pay three pounds—six months' salary—to come and work in South Africa.

Gandhi took up the Indian cause with tireless energy. He wrote letters to newspapers, organized protests and petitions, and founded a campaign group, the Natal Indian Congress, to fight for Indians' rights.

Gandhi was determined to improve the lives of Indian workers in South Africa, such as those pictured below.

Gandhi as a young lawyer and campaigner in South Africa, when he still wore Western clothes.

"Thus the lynching ultimately proved to be a blessing for me." Gandhi on being beaten up by an anti-Indian mob. He forgave his attackers and called for them to be spared from punishment, which increased public sympathy for him.

Gandhi's law career in Pretoria was going well, but he was also known for his political activities. Returning from a trip to India in 1897, he was met by an angry crowd at the docks. They beat him and pelted him with bricks and rotten fish, claiming he intended to flood South Africa with Indians.

Gandhi was almost beaten to death, but was saved by the police. After the incident, the press supported his campaign and he grew more popular than ever among the Indians in South Africa.

The Simple Life

Over the years, Gandhi improved life for Indians in South Africa. At the same time, he began to make changes in his own life, gradually converting himself into the simply dressed, monk-like figure he is remembered as today.

He began by cutting his own hair and cleaning his own bathroom. According to Hindu tradition, these tasks should only be performed by Untouchables—the lowest members of society.

Gandhi in South Africa in 1914, wearing a cotton tunic—the first version of his famous plain white robes.

Gandhi (bottom right) set up this ashram, a kind of communal farm, near the city of Johannesburg. There he and his followers ate simply, prayed, studied, and shared everyday tasks.

At first, Gandhi's wife, Kasturbai, did not approve, but he asked her to do the same. He fed his family on a basic diet of fruit and nuts and he often fasted completely. He also began to wear plain white clothes.

After reading the works of philosophers such as John Ruskin and Henry Thoreau, Gandhi developed the idea of winning political battles through nonviolent civil disobedience. He used the term *Satyagraha*, meaning "truth-force," to describe this approach and encouraged Indians in South Africa to use it in their campaigns.

"Satyagraha has been designed as an effective substitute for violence."
Gandhi describing his new idea of *Satyagraha*, an approach involving civil disobedience and the constant search for truth and peace.

Back to India

In 1914, Gandhi negotiated new conditions for Indians with General Jan Smuts, the South African prime minister. Indian marriages, which had been made unlawful, were made legal again, and the charge for working in South Africa was abolished. Gandhi and Kasturbai decided it was time to go home to India. Gandhi was forty-four—more than halfway through his life.

Having proved himself as a campaigner in South Africa, Gandhi now had a new cause. He wanted independence for India.

Gandhi and his wife, Kasturbai, in Bombay (now called Mumbai) in 1915, soon after they arrived back in India. Kasturbai now agreed with her husband's ideas and was loyal to his simple lifestyle.

"Not only is Swaraj our birthright, but it is our sacred duty to win it."
Gandhi talking about the need for *Swaraj*—or independence—for India.

Gandhi addressing an outdoor meeting of his countrymen in Calcutta in May 1919. At this early stage in his career, Gandhi still occasionally wore British-style clothing.

Soon after his return in 1915 he began to travel the country, protesting against British rule and calling for *Swaraj* (independence). He fought for better conditions for poor weavers and went on a fast until he won them a wage increase. He also set up a new communal farm, or ashram, near Ahmadabad. Gandhi and some of his followers stayed here, living simply and sharing work equally.

Traditional Hindu society has a caste system which places people at different levels, or *jati*. At the bottom of the pile are the Untouchables, who have to do all the worst jobs and are considered too unclean to touch. Gandhi had always questioned this idea, even as a child. Despite the protests of some of his followers, Gandhi welcomed Untouchables into the ashram to show that he believed all people were equal.

The Great Soul

While traveling around India, Gandhi visited a school run by the great Indian poet Rabindranath Tagore. It was Tagore who gave Gandhi the nickname Mahatma, which means "Great Soul" in the ancient Indian language, Sanskrit. From then on he was known as Mahatma Gandhi, as he is still known today.

"I have never, even in my dream, thought that I was Mahatma and that others were Alpatma [little souls]." Gandhi modestly denying that the title "Mahatma" had made him conceited.

Gandhi in later life with his friend, the poet Rabindranath Tagore. Tagore taught students at his school to dance and weave flower garlands. Gandhi thought they should be doing more useful tasks, such as cleaning the toilets.

During World War I (1914–1918), Indian soldiers fought in the British army in Europe. After the war, many Indians felt India deserved to be granted independence in return for its help.

Gandhi knew that *Satyagraha* and civil disobedience could help to win independence. He urged ordinary Indians to become *Satyagrahi*, or followers of the truth, and called on them to resist British rule by going on strike. News of his hunger strikes and protest speeches spread across the country by word of mouth, radio, and newspaper reports. Huge crowds gathered in peaceful protest at some of India's holiest sites.

In 1919, British troops fired on a crowd of peaceful protesters in Amritsar, killing over 300 people. Gandhi was horrified. He called off the strikes, determined to win independence without bloodshed.

This picture shows Indian soldiers in the British army in France, during World War I (1914–1918).

The Cloth Campaign

By 1920, Gandhi was famous. He spoke to huge crowds numbering hundreds of thousands, encouraging them not to pay British taxes or wear British clothes. This was the beginning of a new campaign called the cloth campaign. The Mahatma urged the public to burn their old British-style clothes and instead spin their own thread on a traditional Indian spinning wheel, or *charkha*.

"The truest test of civilization, culture, and dignity is character, not clothing." Gandhi pointing out, during his cloth campaign, that modern Western clothes did not make their wearers better than anyone else.

Gandhi spinning his own khadi (cloth) on a charkha (spinning wheel). He now described himself as a "farmer and weaver," not a lawyer.

By the end of 1919, Gandhi had joined forces with the official independence movement, the Indian National Congress. The group adopted the *charkha* as its symbol. When violence broke out again in 1922, Gandhi was arrested and imprisoned.

Gandhi during a fast in 1924, which he began as a protest against the violence between Hindus and Muslims. The girl in the picture is Indira Gandhi, who later became India's prime minister. She was not Gandhi's daughter, but the daughter of his friend Jawaharlal Nehru.

When he was released two years later, the movement had died down. Gandhi revived it with more demonstrations and speaking tours and went on another hunger strike to stop fighting between Hindus and Muslims. Unlike Hindus, who believe in many gods, Muslims believe there is only one god, whose name is Allah. Since Hindus and Muslims shared many of the same areas of India, there was often tension between them. In 1925, Gandhi was elected president of the Indian National Congress.

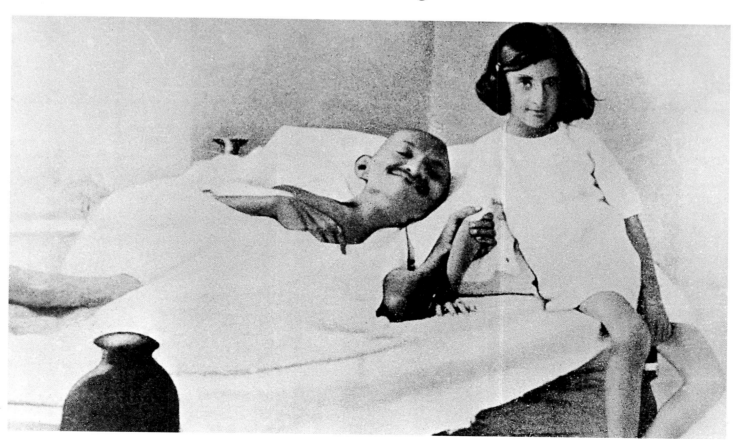

India Unites

A protest march through the streets of Bombay (now Mumbai) in 1930. The women in the procession are wearing white homespun clothes and carrying signs urging people to boycott British goods.

Gandhi was now almost 60 years old and had a new nickname, *Bapu*, which means "Grandpa." Everyone in India knew who he was and millions were joining in with his civil disobedience campaign. They refused to buy British goods or pay taxes, went on strike from their jobs, and attended huge rallies to hear Gandhi speak.

"Non-cooperation with evil is as much a duty as cooperation with good." Gandhi justifying the principle of non-cooperation and civil disobedience.

24

Gandhi in front of a crowd of protestors. Sometimes he made a speech, but sometimes he simply stood in silence with his hands together, inspiring the crowd with this simple demonstration of peaceful protest.

However, "Bapu" was suffering from exhaustion. He had given up the presidency of the Indian National Congress at the end of 1925 and was often unwell. He was also upset when anti-British riots broke out, as they often did. He still wanted a completely nonviolent victory.

Finally, the viceroy (British controller) of India, Baron Irwin, agreed to meet with Gandhi. But Irwin's hands were tied, since the British government would not grant him the power to give in to Indian demands. In the end, Gandhi and the Indian National Congress decided to declare independence themselves, on December 31, 1929.

The Salt Struggle

"We are marching in the name of God."
Gandhi talking to newspaper reporters during the salt march.

Although the Congress had declared independence, the British government did not agree, and the boycotts and riots continued. So Gandhi began planning a new *Satyagraha*, which was to become his most famous struggle.

On March 12, 1930, Gandhi and a group of followers set off from his ashram, the communal farm where he lived near Ahmadabad. They were heading for the coast. As they walked, Gandhi preached his beliefs, urging people to spin their own cloth, avoid meat and alcohol, and disobey the British. They gathered supporters on the way and when they reached Dandi there were thousands of marchers.

When Gandhi bent and picked up the first handful of salt from Dandi beach, he sent a message around the world that Indians would no longer bow to British laws.

Gandhi leading the famous salt march, accompanied by supporters and friends.

In this picture, Gandhi's followers are making salt by putting seawater in dishes to evaporate in the sun.

Across the country, people began collecting their own salt instead of buying heavily taxed salt from the British—which they were supposed to do by law. There were more riots, protests, and arrests, but the salt march worked. Gandhi was imprisoned for starting the campaign, but after his release the following year he was invited to Britain to take part in independence talks.

A riot in the streets of Calcutta, in eastern India, sparked by Gandhi's release from prison in early 1931.

Gandhi in Britain

Gandhi went to Britain in 1931 to take part in a conference on Indian independence. Many British people were in favor of granting India its freedom and the government had decided to address the question.

However, the trip was really more useful for Gandhi as a publicity exercise. The British press and public loved him, and his visit was reported around the world. He made a speech in Oxford, visited factory workers, met the film star Charlie Chaplin, and had tea with King George V—all dressed in his usual white robes.

This picture shows Gandhi with the film star Charlie Chaplin at the house of an Indian friend in London.

Gandhi greeted by a crowd of supporters and journalists as he emerged from a taxi in London in 1931.

Gandhi with British workers on a visit to Lancashire in England.

"My love of the British is equal to that of my own people."
Gandhi on the British.

The conference itself was not such a success. It was impossible to work out how to divide up power between different groups—especially Hindus and Muslims—in a new, independent India.

Meanwhile, India had a new viceroy, Lord Willingdon, who was clamping down on all protests and boycotts. Not long after returning from his triumphant trip to Britain, Gandhi found himself in jail again.

The Untouchables

While Gandhi was in prison he learned that if independence did go ahead, the British government planned to hold separate elections for the Untouchables, the social outcasts at the bottom of Indian society.

Gandhi photographed during one of his many fasts. This picture shows how thin his beliefs and way of life had made him.

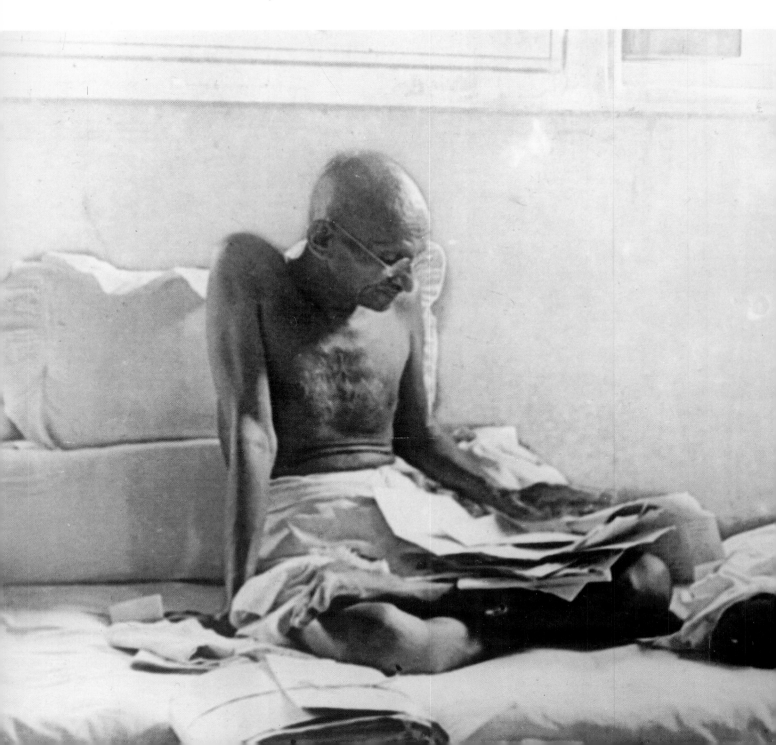

"Untouchability poisons Hinduism as a drop of arsenic poisons milk." Gandhi on Untouchability. He believed all people were worthy of respect and hated the idea that anyone should be labeled "untouchable."

An untouchable woman at work in Delhi, India, in the early 20th century.

He welcomed Untouchables (whom he called *harijans*, meaning "Children of God") into his home, and even adopted a *harijan* girl, Lakshmi, as his daughter.

In September 1932, Gandhi decided to support the Untouchables by going on a hunger strike to force the British to change their plans. For a week he refused all food and drink and grew close to death. His state of health was headline news all over India and the taboos of the caste system were broken as high caste and *harijan* people ate and waited together.

Finally, the British gave in and Gandhi lived. However, the caste system itself was not destroyed so easily, and Untouchability still exists today.

A Break from Politics

When Gandhi came out of prison in 1933, he decided to leave politics for a while. He gave his ashram to the Untouchables and in 1934 resigned as a member of the Indian National Congress. He left his friend Jawaharlal Nehru, the new Congress leader, to manage the political campaign and became a wandering traveler again.

Gandhi speaking at a conference in Calcutta in 1934.

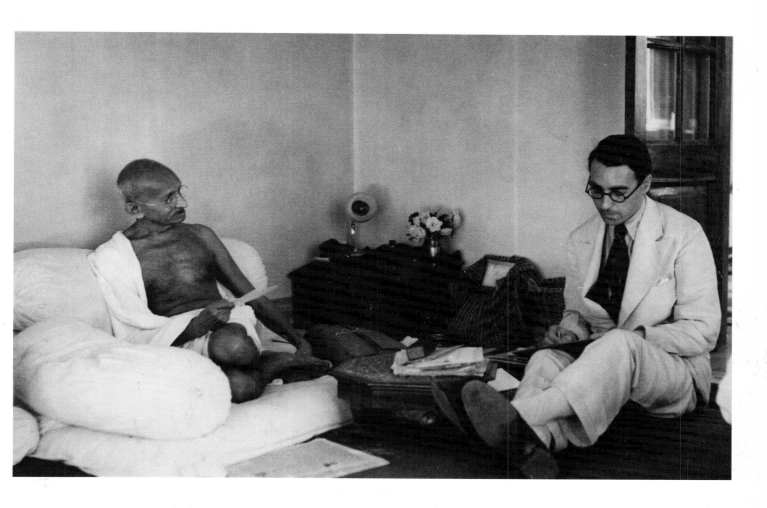

*Gandhi being interviewed by Robert Stimson, a journalist for **Picture Post**, in 1940. By this time Gandhi's name was known throughout the world.*

This time, however, he was world famous and followers and reporters came from around the globe to see him. He promised his friends that he would return to politics when he felt the time was right.

In 1939, World War II broke out. Gandhi used his powerful voice to call for nonviolence, but to no effect.

As a British territory, India was an important barrier between Germany and its Japanese allies. The Indian National Congress promised to support the war effort in return for independence as soon as the war ended. Many world leaders urged Britain to agree, but the new British prime minister, Winston Churchill, hated the thought of losing India from the British Empire.

"Never give in. Never. Never. Never. Never." Prime Minister Winston Churchill's attitude toward giving up any of Great Britain's former colonies.

"Quit India!"

In April 1942, in the middle of the war, Gandhi decided to start campaigning again. His new slogan was "Quit India!," and he called for an immediate, nonviolent revolution. But he and the leaders of the Indian National Congress soon found themselves in prison yet again, while rioting, terrorism, and police violence increased across India.

Gandhi at the flower-strewn deathbed of his wife, Kasturbai, in 1944.

This was an enormous disappointment for Gandhi, as he longed for a peaceful, nonviolent outcome. His misery was worsened in 1944 when Kasturbai, who had stood by him for 62 years, caught acute bronchitis. He was allowed to leave jail briefly to visit her deathbed, and she died in his arms. Gandhi then became ill himself. Churchill, sure he was about to die, had him released from jail.

"I cannot imagine life without Ba...her passing has left a vacuum which will never be filled."
Gandhi on the death of his wife Kasturbai, who had been nicknamed "Ba"("Mother") by the Indian people.

But there was light at the end of the tunnel. Gandhi survived, the war ended, and a new Labor government came to power in Britain. One of its priorities was to arrange independence for India.

Left: *Gandhi on his way to an Indian National Congress committee meeting. Despite his grief at Kasturbai's death, he continued to work toward independence for India.*

Right: *Gandhi with Jawaharlal Nehru, his close friend and political ally, who became leader of the Indian National Congress.*

Independence at Last

Britain was ready to leave India and let Indians rule themselves. But no one could agree on exactly how the country should be run. A conference was held in Simla in 1945 to discuss the problem, but it didn't help. Britain wanted to give power to the mainly Hindu Indian National Congress, led by Jawaharlal Nehru. But Ali Jinnah, leader of a Muslim organization called the Muslim League, wanted India's Muslims to have their own, "pure" Muslim state.

After the conference, Hindus and Muslims all over India began fighting and killing each other. Gandhi, who did not believe that one religion was better than any other, went on the road again making speeches and calling for the violence to stop.

Ali Jinnah, the Muslim leader who demanded a new, separate country for India's Muslims. That country was Pakistan, which was founded when India became independent.

36

> "God is not in Kaaba or in Kashi. He is within every one of us."
> Gandhi on religious unrest in India. He believed that all religions were really the same and shared the same God. (Kaaba is a Muslim holy site and Kashi is a Hindu holy site. Both are in India.)

Violence between Hindus and Muslims swept India in the late 1940s. This photo shows riots in Bombay in 1946.

Finally, in 1947, the British government made a decision. Britain would leave India by June 1948. There was still no solution, but it would have to be sorted out in time.

Partition

Ali Jinnah, the leader of the Muslim League, was determined to establish a separate country for the Muslims. He threatened to start a civil war if his demands weren't met. India was about to be divided.

Sooner than expected, on August 15, 1947, the Indian National Congress acted. They raised the new Indian flag (a modified version of the Indian National Congress flag) in Delhi, India's capital. Nehru made an independence speech,

"We Indians are one as no two Englishmen are." Gandhi opposing Partition. He saw India as a united whole and couldn't bear the idea of Indians turning against one another.

This map shows the movement of Muslims and Hindus during Partition. Other places mentioned in this book are also shown.

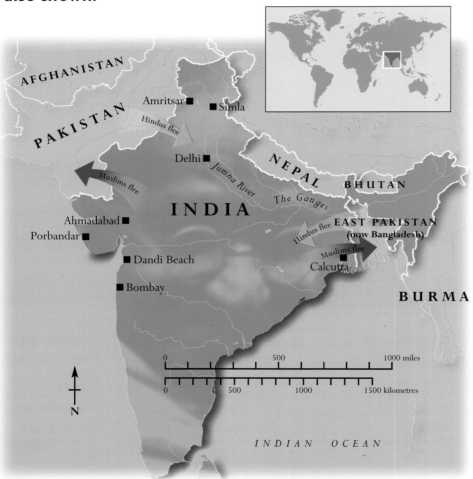

but Gandhi was nowhere to be seen. He had gone to Calcutta, still on his mission to stop Hindu–Muslim riots.

Thousands of Muslims began streaming toward the mainly Muslim northwest corner of India, which (along with what is now Bangladesh) was to become Pakistan. Meanwhile, Hindus trapped in the new "pure" Muslim state fled back to India. This process, which took place in the later months of 1947, was known as Partition. Over a million people lost their lives in the fighting between Muslims and Hindus. Gandhi, the nonviolent revolutionary, was devastated.

Muslims cling to a refugee train heading for Pakistan shortly after Partition. Trains taking Muslims and Hindus to their new homes were often attacked by the opposing side.

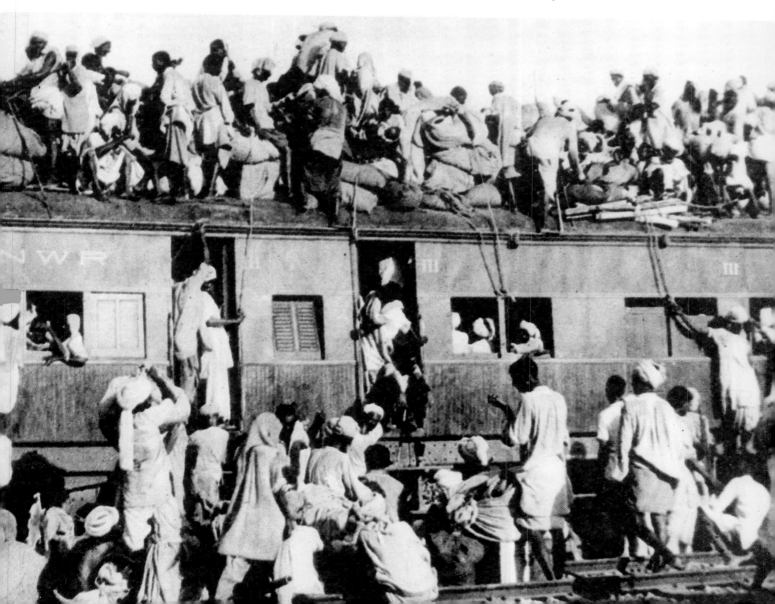

A Violent Death

Gandhi had managed to calm the riots in Calcutta and returned to Delhi, where he stayed with a friend. He continued to call for peace between religions and even fasted again to try to stop the fighting. But many Hindus and Muslims turned against him, each accusing him of supporting the other side. On January 20, 1948, a bomb was thrown at the house where he was staying. Gandhi was unhurt, but the message was clear.

Gandhi with his grandnieces Abha and Manu. After his wife's death, they were his assistants and constant companions.

Just ten days later, on January 30, Gandhi walked out of his house to go to a prayer meeting along with his two grandnieces, Abha and Manu. In the crowd waiting for him was Nathuram Godse, a Hindu newspaper editor and strong supporter of the Hindus.

Suddenly Godse darted out of the crowd and pushed past Manu. He took out a pistol and shot Gandhi three times. According to witnesses, Gandhi sank to the ground, breathing the words "*He Rama*"—meaning "Oh God"—before he died.

Nathuram Godse (front row, right) in the dock, accused of killing Gandhi. With him are eight other men accused of taking part in the plan to murder the Mahatma.

"Death is at any time blessed, but it is twice blessed for a warrior who dies for his cause, that is, truth." Gandhi on death. He was 78 at the time of his death.

Farewell to "Bapu"

Gandhi's friend Jawaharlal Nehru was now independent India's first prime minister. As soon as he heard of Gandhi's death he rushed to Delhi, and that evening he announced the news on India's national radio station. The whole country was plunged into mourning.

Gandhi's ashes are carried to the Ganges River on a decorated chariot, surrounded by mourners.

"*The light has gone out of our lives, and there is darkness everywhere.... Our beloved leader, Bapu, as we call him, the Father of our Nation, is no more.*"
Jawaharlal Nehru broadcasting the news of Gandhi's assassination on January 30, 1948.

Indian cabinet ministers set sail to scatter Gandhi's ashes on the holy waters of the Ganges and Jumna rivers.

Godse, Gandhi's assassin, had not tried to escape. He was quickly arrested and pleaded guilty to the killing, for which he was eventually executed.

Gandhi was given a traditional Hindu funeral. His body was washed, covered with flowers, and carried through the streets to a sandalwood funeral pyre, where a crowd of over two million people watched it burn. Ten days later, the ashes were scattered at the meeting point of India's two holiest rivers, the Ganges and the Jumna.

Gandhi's Legacy

Today, Gandhi is remembered around the world. His distinctive appearance has made him one of the most easily recognized leaders of all time. But what exactly did he leave behind?

Although he is sometimes treated like a saint, Gandhi did not see himself as a religious leader. And although he led India to independence, he was not a politician. He didn't even achieve his aims—India's independence came at a terrible cost in violence and suffering.

Nelson Mandela, who campaigned for racial freedom in South Africa, was awarded the Gandhi Peace Prize in the year 2000. Many people thought Gandhi should have won the Nobel Peace Prize, although he never did. After his death, the Indian government set up the Gandhi Peace Prize in his honor.

Yet Gandhi showed the world how effective nonviolent protest could be. His philosophy of love, peace, and forgiveness between people of different religions, races, and beliefs has inspired many struggles for freedom around the world. And his words of wisdom, preserved in his writings and recalled by his friends, continue to inspire us today.

This statue of Gandhi on his salt march stands in the center of New Delhi, India.

"Where there is love, there is life; hatred leads to destruction." One of Gandhi's most famous quotations, summing up his belief in nonviolence, forgiveness, and the power of love.

45

Glossary

Aristocrat A member of the elite or ruling classes.

Ashram A communal dwelling founded by a spiritual leader.

Boycott To refuse to buy goods or services as a way of making a protest.

Campaign A series of protests and activities designed to bring about change.

Caste system A traditional Hindu hereditary social system that divides society into many different levels, or *jati*.

Charkha An Indian spinning wheel.

Civil disobedience Refusal to obey the laws or commands of the government.

Civil war A war between two groups inside the same country.

Curfew A ban on going outdoors, usually imposed at night.

Fast To go without food for a certain period of time.

Harijan Gandhi's name for Untouchables. The word means "Children of God."

Hindu A member of the Hindu religion. Hindus believe in many different gods.

Jati *see* Caste system.

Khadi An Indian word for plain, homespun cloth.

Lynch To kill someone as a punishment, without the approval of the law.

Mahatma A Sanskrit (ancient Indian) word that means "Great Soul."

Muslim A member of Islam, a religion that has one God.

Petition A written request to the government, often signed by many people.

Philosopher A person who thinks deeply about what life means.

Pyre A bonfire for burning a dead body.

Satyagraha A word invented by Gandhi to describe nonviolent, peaceful resistance. It translates as "truth-force."

Strike To refuse to work as a form of protest.

Swaraj An Indian word for independence.

Terrorism Violent and illegal acts performed to protest against laws or attitudes.

Untouchables The lowest members of society, according to the caste system.

Vaishya The *jati* or caste "level" that Gandhi was born into.

Viceroy Someone who rules in place of a monarch. A British viceroy governed India when it was in the British Empire.

Further Information

Books to Read

Bains, Rae. *Gandhi: Peaceful Warrior (Easy Biographies)*. Mahwah, NJ: Troll Associates, 1990.

Demi. *Gandhi.* New York: Margaret McElderry (Simon and Schuster Children's Publishing), 2001.

Mitchell, Pratima. *Gandhi: The Father of Modern India (What's Their Story).* New York: Oxford University Press, 1998.

Date Chart

October 2, 1869 Mohandas Karamchand Gandhi born in Porbandar, Porbandar State, India.

1882 Marries Kasturbai Makanji in an arranged Hindu wedding.

1885 Gandhi's father dies. His own first child is born, but dies a few days later.

1888 Gandhi's son Harilal is born.

1888 Goes to London to study law.

1891 Returns to India as a qualified lawyer.

1892 Gandhi's son Manilal is born.

April 1893 Sails to South Africa to work as a lawyer and encounters racial prejudice during a train journey.

1894 Founds the Natal Indian Congress to fight for the rights of Indians in South Africa.

1897 Gandhi's son Ramdas is born.

1900 Gandhi's son Devadas is born.

1903 Builds first ashram near Durban, South Africa.

1906 Develops concept of *Satyagraha*, or truth-force.

September 1913 Leads final South African campaign, resulting in improved conditions for Indian workers.

1915 Returns to India with family. Founds a new ashram near Ahmedabad and becomes a wandering traveler.

1918 Fasts in order to win rights for Ahmedabad textile workers.

1920 Begins nationwide campaign urging people to boycott British goods and weave their own cloth.

1922–1924 Spends two years in jail.

1925 Elected president of Indian National Congress.

1929 Indian National Congress declares India independent without British consent.

1930 Leads "salt march" to gather salt illegally from the beach at Dandi.

1932 Fasts in order to win rights for Untouchables.

1934 Resigns from Indian National Congress and travels around India.

1942 Launches "Quit India" campaign and urges Britain to grant India independence. He is immediately sent to jail.

1944 Gandhi's wife Kasturbai dies. He becomes ill and is released from jail.

1947 Britain agrees to grant India full independence and promises to leave the country by June 1948. Gandhi goes to Calcutta to campaign against violent riots.

August 15, 1947 The Indian National Congress raises a new Indian flag in Delhi.

1947 Over a million die as the country is divided into India and Pakistan.

January 30, 1948 Gandhi is shot dead in Delhi by Nathuram Godse.

Index

All numbers in **bold** refer to pictures accompanying the text.

© 2002 White-Thomson Publishing Ltd